Rivers of Living Water

Poems from 2024

Cover design by Iqra Qutub.

Author contact: nate@wagramorchard.com

CONTENTS

RHYMED VERSES

SPRINGTIME JEZEBEL

From a year of spartan showers
Take a steamy soak.
From a hundred hungry hours
Smell the cooking smoke.
From the wind and thorns and splinters
Rest and breathe a spell.
From a dozen virgin winters,
Springtime jezebel.
From a skimpy way of being
Take a break awhile;
Find a sight that's worth the seeing;
Make a warmer smile.

RIGHT AND WRONG

The left side of my jaw was struck,
Becoming sore and feeling frail.
My left knee lost its loyal strength;
Athleticism stalled and failed.

Maybe I was the milk drinker,
The clueless infant after all.
Maybe I was the lame laggard;
After my march of pride, a fall.

Maybe this is the right reply
When left-side uses fail me now.
I know nothing. I've been so wrong,
Although it's all been right somehow.

THE TEMPLE OF AMOS

The temple of Amos is empty now
Without mind, without spirit;
No breath, no music, no ear to hear it.

The temple of Amos is frigid now
Without warmth, without vigor.
The void he left remains, growing bigger.

The temple of Amos is earthbound now
Beneath grass, in low places,
No more to view the sun, nor our faces.

The temple of Amos is silent now
Without jokes, without laughter,
His voice away somewhere in hereafter.

The temple of Amos is hidden now.
Amos Crew, strong and true,
The youth is gone—dear God, what to do?

The temple of Amos is memory now
And in floods came our weeping.
Though emptied out, this vigil I'm keeping.

The temple of Amos is faded now
Without beat, without action,
Cut down and stripped of purpose and passion.

The temple of Amos—its fall cut deep.
Out flowed blood, tears, and letters;
This echo of Heledd—lamenting our betters.

The temple of Amos is humus now.
Shallow shadows now hover
Where once he stood, the best baby brother.

PAIN AND A POND

A pain became a spade

And dug, and cut, and hurt.

A rain filled in the hole it made

And patted down the dirt.

The spade was set aside

And sun came out to shine.

The hardened hole was fully dried.

An empty form was mine.

And then a brighter cloud

Of purple evening storm

Came pouring, thundering so loud,

And joy filled up the form.

MAN TO BOY

In Spring is when the blessed grin
Will break,
The sacred laughing dawn begin
To make
The smiling line curve up and out
To joy.
In Spring, the winter man is now
A boy.

KNEELING

My muse, she was silent a terrible while.

Her lips wouldn't open, not even to smile.

Obeying her silence, I wrote not a line,

Though craving a taste of her sensual wine.

No, all her old cellars were dry as a bone

And hollow were all those connections I'd
    known.

Routines were threadbare, simple joys petered
    out,

And sunsets were boring—no color nor cloud.

A father and husband can't get up and go

And find some inspiring adventure, you know;

Diseases transmitted and loyalties lost

Will ruin your wandering, run up the cost.

For better or worse, her cold shoulder for days

Was chilling, till she said one little word:
　　"Praise."

Like thunder it hit me, the hymn I had missed,

The prayer I'd evaded, the kneeling I'd dissed.

I'll bow to the Being of which we're all part.

The poem named "You" is the core of my heart.

YOU

You sing to me.

You sing through me.

You're in me and I'm in you.

You're all singing.

You're my tingling.

You're a sense that dawned and grew.

You're the oak tree.

You're the grass leaf.

You're the smoke and morning dew.

You're the hurting

And the curing,

Fleeing and returning, too.

You're a flying.

You're a dying.

Air and emptiness, both you.

You're the ocean,

Dancing motion.

Drink this wine and taste of you.

You're a spinning.

You're a grinning.

Losing all is winning you.

You're the smile

Of a child.

You're a wrestling I knew.

You're desire;

You're the fire;

Every ash and calorie, you.

You're my eyesight,

Brighter sunlight,

Color tutor, visual cue.

You're the body,

Though ungodly.

Each and all expand from you.

You're the giving

And receiving,

Out and in and weaving through.

You're the question,

Wordless lesson.

The eternal Word is you.

Words like "you" and

"Me" are shorthand

For what's unified and true.

You're the Mother,

Father, brother,

Subtler kinships old and new.

Silent breathing,

Rhythm beating,

Elohim, Adonai, *Duw* —

Names all miss you.

We misplace you.

There's no claiming I can do.

You're the lightning,

Big and frightening.

Rain, refresh, reclaim, renew.

Every rainbow,

Each moon halo,

Every sacred midnight: you.

Every goodness,

Fun and kindness

Flows original from you.

You're the living,

The forgiving.

All my saving grace is You.

TONIGHT

Tonight I won't listen to thoughts,
What things are or might have been.
I'll thoughtlessly gaze at your face,
See your tone and sense your skin.

Tonight all the stars and the moon
On your forehead come to rest.
They drink in two bottomless ponds
Where the water is the best.

Tonight I don't care about work,
What to do or games to win.
A universe lives in your lips
And a goddess holds your chin.

RIVERBANK

All they can do, these lines,

    Is at the very most

    Bring you down to the riverbank

However many times.

If you're a friend you'll dive,

    Leaving the lines behind.

    Laughing, see where the water flows

When you become alive.

SKYSCRAPING ASSUMPTIONS

It wasn't easy reading between

The logic lines of Saint Augustine.

He stacked his castles, scraped the sky

So bravely that I wondered why

So many of his answers leaned

Too hard on high assumptions, it seemed.

THE LEAST OF THESE

What if another expanded level may feature

    Other brethren-to-be?

"What you have done to the least of these my creatures

    You have done unto me."

Maybe a river's released from sacred sayings

    We can finally see.

"What you have done to the least of these my rivers

    You have done unto me."

Maybe a fulness unleashed in holy words

    Is a meaning for me.

"What you have done to the least of these,

    My groves, my acres, my sisters,

    You have done unto me."

ARRIVAL TIME

Did others hum, salute the sun
    For endless aching ages past?
Have others kissed a silver moon
    Time to time always?
Were verses of the vales of death
    Strung on ancient lines to last?
Did all-embracing joy-songs mark
    Immemorial days?
Very well, let me arrive
Late to endless marches streaming
Unmoderated, uncensored, unblocked
With every line that led to here;
Unequalled for a time, releasing,
Imbibing many others now,
    Encapsulating, surrounding,
    Expanding, rounding out,
    Resounding All in every one,

Humming an old, old tune.

A body lean, a spirit clean

Foot in the earth

Eye to the sun

See the near-unseen

Hand giving birth

Undo what's been done

SACRED MIDNIGHT

Lying on my back out here
Looking into space, a tear
Dribbles down the temple to the ear.

Under me the ground is cold.
Midnight's quiet. Souls unfold.
Openings out here cannot be told.

Something's drifting in the air
Reaching here from everywhere
Bringing steeper meaning to "aware".

Who will come and share this scene?
What does friendship really mean?
Who will be here, breathing in this dream?

EVERYWHERE

Look in my eye. I swear
I see God everywhere.
Sometimes it's all too much,
Too wonderful to touch.

You're the man. It's your turn.
Turn the world. Feel the burn,
Seeing the Woman right,
Making for God a sight.

Meeting your eye, I swear
I meet God everywhere.
Sometimes it's all too deep,
Too beautiful to sleep.

SET FREE

A younger form of me,
Flames in the eyes,
Wrote down some tripe;
Hot words I thought to be
Buoyant and wise,
"A man's way of life."

Then deeper ways of life
Came crackling through
In static lines,
Dividing like a knife
Through all I knew,
Submerging my mind.

Now nine times out of ten,
Try as I might,
All I can see

For women or for men

Is doing right

Equals love-set-free.

ACCEPTING

A scattered, spread-out new unity
A solitude of community
    There, far out on a limb
    Bare, out sunning the skin
Though I'm barely sorry
Feel free to forgive me
    If my flesh in its youth
    Spilled too much of its truth
But here we've entered past a portal
We sang the flesh, enjoyed the mortal

Now, woman, I see your sea foam
And call you my sister, or daughter, or mother
And man, I know your longing to roam
May you be my brother, a son or a father
    And you who hover ambiguously
    I smile—your confusion won't agitate me

I'll call you a sibling, or maybe my child

My welcome is easy, my judgement is
mild

Your diet may suffer, your hormones
may cry

Come share in my supper, sleep under
this sky

The woods our cathedral, the clouds are a dome

Here echoing timeless, accepting each other

Here learning of kindness, of kin, of home

Cut off from our nature

Is where we go wrong

Our Mother, she knows us

We wander so long

But here's an old flavor

Sung in a new tone

Embracing thy neighbor

Accepting thine own

CONVINCEMENT TIME

A light inside

Deep centered down

A seed within

The ground

Convincement time

A silent tune

Could not arrive

Too soon

And not too late

A need to roam

To learn to wait

For Home

STUNNED

What could follow such a feeling?
What could follow such a sight?
Thunder leaves you deaf and reeling,
Stunned and still like dead of night.

> Then they rise
> Up again,
> Moving skies
> Showing when
> It's the time,
> Shining in.
> The old line
> Shall begin.

Where to go on such a morning?
In, where glory swept the room,
Or outside to watch the forming
Of a morning full in bloom.

IN-BETWEEN VERSES

PEACE AND PASSION

Peace is the root.
Joy is the branches.
Passion, the blossoms
And love, the fruit.

The solid central stalk,
The trunk from taproot to tippy top,
Is a radiant upward flow
Of the Great Spirit....

Hold that thought.
May I tuck this blossom
Behind your ear?

THREE RUBY DROPS

Three ruby drops escape
This living gift to you my brethren
Which bled out from a chest agape.
And these, no squeezings of
A dry belaboring Spinoza,
But easy, easy to slip down
To sibling destinations
Via salty fluid lines.
My beloved, my nation,
Be even closer kin of mine
When destinations of your mind
Are triune and divine,
Are Gratitude, Love, Unity.
All else falls in line and stops
Beneath this holy trinity,
These three, these ruby drops.

SIMMER

Come dip a tin pot
Sit and sip with me
Soup never came from a
Rootless tumbleweed
Look how the Big Dipper evokes
A Johnny Appleseed
And wandering's a real itch
Feels oh-so-good to scratch
May orbit your whole 20s and 30s
Before sore hunger sits down to
Simmer with this melting pot
Slow-cooking out all thought
See constellations rooted
  To this one spot

FRONTIER BATTLE

On the frontier there

Counterattacking, they come,

Cheeky, fearless pair:

Greenbriar and Chickasaw Plum.

In the gleam of a heavenly areola,

A glowing ring overhead,

Impossible tangles recover a field like ghostly
    fingers

On harp strings of humming affirmation.

Now a shadow's back,

Leafy umbrella's remade

Where a sneak attack

Planted the flag of the shade.

EXPLORER ITCH

Oh, to be a wanderer in

A world not conquered by concrete;

To be an explorer, but without

Empire's tentacles following in the wake.

Oh, to be untethered, light and free

And young and naïve forever,

Tending gardens of fleeting discovery.

> But the world is heavily captured.

> Rules and empires smother it all,

> And knowledge encumbers adulthood,

> And Adam and Eve repeatedly fall.

That's how it plays for a season.

Oh, to see the seasons change.

SEE?

Shove off from the harbor.

Embark from the pier,

From firmness to water,

From doer to seer.

      I wish you could've seen—

      Seen in it—

      Seen into its color.

      I wish you could've seen it with

      Eyes that aren't eyes,

      Seen that light as it glances,

      As it dances still across the ripples.

It held its own meaning;

It was it, you see.

No squinting or leaning

Will help. Only be.

      Did time hurry you along?

      Did time come—

Did time stop—

I mean, was duration relevant at all?

Either you're moving or not,

Moved or not,

Will arrive or not.

See?

SENTIENT BEINGS

Sentient beings, can't we help ourselves

I play my time in sensuous mind

Merry-go-rounds of kicks

Sights and scents of hedonistic

Openings

To what ends, though

When it bends to

"Be still and..."

No

Wrapped in our wings, we attach ourselves

Open new minds to pass the time

Shake a sharing sensing out

Loosening

I drank the wine

Following each his line

Fulfilling each her prime

Coming to reach

To climb the vine

The Vine

"...and know..."

Wings weigh down with

Attachments over time

"...know that I Am..."

Sentient beings, can't we help

Can't We

Feel the real work

Kick in

Till it tends to

Detach

Ourself

THE DAIMON IN THE EYE

Some sights will fly

    Fresh and laughing there,

        Cool and bright and fleeting

Like inner flesh

    Of a prickly pear;

A sonorous mosaic rolled across the horizon,

Billowing incantation

Of flickering rumbling clouds

    All shot through with heated hues,

        Melek Taus with tail feathers
        spread.

I saw a girl today,

Curls flying behind her,

Sleek of form, skipping and jogging,

A little swirling scarf-like thing

    Comprising half her brilliant clothing.

Heaven knows I likely need a teacher,

For the daimon in the eye baffles me,

Speaking chiefly through pain

Or else in sights like these.

BROUGHT-IN WATER

Brought-in water will keep them alive
Though only by rain can they thrive and grow
And growth is how to survive, you know

Brought-in books and saved-up words
Can siphon life in a momentary way
Though only purple rain can save the day

RIVERS OF LIVING WATER

In between the paper covers
Underneath the moving waters
Other things all fade before
Beginningless and endless Now
Seeking melts into the found
Seed resolves in fertile ground
Afterlife gives way to Life
And finished writings fade
Covered over in fulfilment
To be filled is to believe
Now where is the man?
His heart will sprout and grow
Who enters this forever
Out of his core will flow
Rivers of living water

UNRHYMED VERSES

NOT THAT INSUFFICIENCY EXISTS

Not that insufficiency exists, but
The best poem can never be read.
The best dance isn't physically feasible.
The best melody is hardly audible.
The best art isn't received with eyes.
And life incessantly strives after itself.
And life dances in the strife as in peace.
And poems are only another color of
Life's love songs to Its own Self.

OUT OF SILENCE

A year or two of total peace
Wasn't yet in the cards.

Thought I'd found the midnight Tao
Of stopping in utter silence
Empty of letters,
And I had,
Though
A flow returns;
Night retreats eternally
In the face of everlasting dawn.

Our souls are too clever to be ruled
Or ever cease from singing sunrise.

FEBRUARY IN THE CHESTNUT FIELD

Brushing against February's ennui

There wave amber straws of

Wild grasses, broomsedge, relieved

Where the puppy loves to sprint around

Golden wisps in relief

Stand against carelessly tinted brambles

Burgundy and purple briars

Dappled in a shiny green

A PRESCRIPTION

Not many answers reside in me.

But I can write you a prescription,

One that will never fail.

After the throes of your greatest grief,

Deepest sorrow of your life,

If the weather is right,

Spend a whole wakeful night or two

Alone in a hardwood forest place

Away from sensations of civilization,

Unafraid to fight through impossible
    canebrakes,

Willing to be still without relief.

And if your food is your silence

And your wine is emptiness of mind,

Looking at nothing but your surroundings,

And toward the sky, earth, your body,

You'll likely hear no rhyme, but

A beat —

Beat –

Beat...

And then —

Then,

You'll begin to see.

TWO HOVERING LIMBS

Is it wavering

Or waving

That spindly tree in wind

Those two hovering limbs

The ones stitching my heart

Are they just wooden

Or reaching

?

EVERY DAY A CHOICE

Every day a choice
A fork, which trail to go for
To be a gentle rain or blizzard
Keystone organism or cancer
Samaritan neighbor or disease
Indigenous or interloper
To be a boon or blight

And every night a sight
For healthy ego's sake
Or in a further deeper trip
To home, to trails where you belong

No two sights will strike you alike
Elusive views may soak to make
A brighter daylight choice

YOU'RE STILL WARM

We went about our routines today,

You and I, shallow habits,

And here's what went unsaid.

You are. And

You are still warm;

Warm with what?

Have we desired too fiercely?

Worked too hard?

Held on too heartily?

Grieved too fiercely, too?

You were born immaculate.

In fulness of time your soul flickered on;

Into existence you streamed full-formed

And there you are,

A mode of life never seen before,

Though familiar still,

Full-fledged confirmation of yourself.

Thank you for being, even for striving.

May many days go by before you flicker to the
    next mode;

Fewer days if your flame is too fierce,

Or if you adore the warmth then more.

Did you think we'd cheat death?

Take control of her timing or form?

Know that she is divine.

Know that you are alive.

Know that healing is wrapped in death.

Though not one of us is safe,

You are still warm.

NEVER ENOUGH

There are never enough words
And words are never enough
And also
There's never enough silence.
Funny how that works,
And funny how
You can never get enough
Of Life.

WRONGS

Trying to

Find the way

How do they go?

The words of kindness

Spoken while standing upon

Layers on layers on layers of wrongs

Crying onion peeling songs

Till kindness fits not

In words at all but

In the way we

Combine

GROVES OF WORDS

Thickets of voiceless shade inside of

Groves of words you've been brought into

Are like an odd forest I found.

Could get lost in these tangles for weeks.

They're not mine, understand,

And yet they're yours now if you like.

"Freely you have received," the Man said,
    "freely give."

And then Pharrell sang it well:

"Happiness is the truth."

The deeper into these woods you go

Beyond the words is real fruit

And goodness falling all around you,

Although,

Doing the happiest things

    Is financially ill-advised.

How can you earn enough daily bread

    While weak from fertile fasting?

How can you step up, perform duties

    After all night awake, alive in the
    groves?

Fine, leave the forest early if you like.

At least I tried to show you it.

MAN

Man, your Y chromosome is
Handed down to you from I-don't-know.
Yet in there where it's seated
Is a knowing.

Every tangible heaven,
Every real beauty eye may see,
Is appointed, anointed,
Light-formed, sacred.

How much brighter, more holy,
Must the Beauty be beyond all touch;
Silent kingdom of fathers,
Elevated.

Every sensible beauty
Enters you, a hazy prism ray

From a heavenly burning
At the center.

In the burning's beginning,
Adam sixty thousand twirls ago
(Earth around her big daddy)
Recreated.

Man, your new recreation
Is a work of bringing back to earth
Light, a kingdom of heaven
From your center.

AN END?

Is this an end of poetry?
Is former music superseded?
Are older sound and sight gone dead?
Is this the end of the lust of the eyes?
The end of the root cellar wine?

If so, good
If not, good
Thy kingdom come
Let these hands be Thy hands

Cupped in expectation
"You have a river to drink," I was told
So where poems were little sips
Or slurping in murky swamps
Then this must be an end

www.ingramcontent.com/pod-product-compliance
Lightning Source LLC
Chambersburg PA
CBHW031236120626
46545CB00003B/1138